His Grace
Through Time and Space

His Grace
Through Time and Space

TRINIDAD RODRIGUEZ

ReadersMagnet, LLC

His Grace Through Time and Space
Copyright © 2023 by Trinidad Rodriguez

Published in the United States of America
ISBN   Paperback: 979-8-89091-179-7
ISBN   eBook: 979-8-89091-180-3

All rights reserved. No part of this publication may be reproduced, stored in a retrieval system or transmitted in any way by any means, electronic, mechanical, photocopy, recording or otherwise without the prior permission of the author except as provided by USA copyright law.

The opinions expressed by the author are not necessarily those of ReadersMagnet, LLC.

ReadersMagnet, LLC
10620 Treena Street, Suite 230 | San Diego, California, 92131 USA
1.619. 354. 2643 | www.readersmagnet.com

Book design copyright © 2023 by ReadersMagnet, LLC. All rights reserved.

Cover design by Ericka Obando
Interior design by Dorothy Lee

TABLE OF CONTENTS

Prologue 7

How Great Thou Art 9

We're All In This Together 16

The Wilderness..22

God Is My Boss..25

Once I Was Blind But Now... 28

God's At Work And Doing Well 30

Daniel 32

Twenty Dollar Bills 37

My Car Won't Go Home 39

I Am The Bell 42

If I Was A Fly On The Wall 46

The Old Ranch On Purgatory Road 48

Three Men Under God's Radar 51

The Man I Can't Forgive...................................56

Released...61

Benevolent Father 65

PROLOGUE

How far back does a story start? How many years from 1942 to 2019? That would be too simple. Subtract 1942 from 2019 is 77. But the question is not a number. It is not the years. It is the lives involved. It is the intricate threads being woven through time and distance... Again, the stories of people. One planned by love, time and distance. What God can stand high enough, to see through a cloud and find the start of two young lives in the future. What God can weave long enough to find the perfect mother with all the unconditional love needed by two little girls. My God who weaves and sees it all and provides for each of us.

For you formed my inward parts;
You covered me in my mother's womb.
I will praise You, for I am fearfully and wonderfully made.
Marvelous are Your works.
And that my soul knows very well.
My frame was not hidden from You.
When I was made in secret.
And skillfully made wrought in the lowest part of the earth,
Your eyes saw my substance, being yet unformed,
And in Your book they all were written.

Unknown

HOW GREAT THOU ART

...whatever you do, do all to the glory of God.
1 CORINTHIANS 10:31

Connecting the dots! Following the path of human lives! Again, my God is alive and touches lives through time and space. Another aha moment on Facebook. I again marvel at **HIS WORK.**

October 2019 I am going through Facebook (social media) and looking at familiar faces of my children, family, friends, and strangers that I don't know. Second look at a faintly familiar face. Do I know this person... Yes...no... yes!

A young Caucasian woman with two children. A picture of the familiar face with two Hispanic girls. The older girl in the picture is wearing a beautiful dress. She is going to her first prom in high school. In the background is her younger sister. The familiar face is identifying the girls as her daughters, they live in Michigan. I start counting back the 1991-92 school year in San Antonio, Texas to October 2019. Twenty-eight years! I had worked in the San Antonio School District in 1991. Then God comes to mind and takes me back to 1990.

I am 48, single mother of three, one grown, one in college, and one in high school. I was out having a girls' night out on a Wednesday night with my coworkers and friends. We had found Mustang Sally in El Paso, a great place for dancing to oldies but goodies music. It was a great place to relieve stress from school and relax. On Wednesdays it was Miller Beer Night and even if I didn't drink, I could have fun. We would dance all night with lots of guys. I ended up dancing with the Miller Man. He was lots of fun and a great dancer and we danced the night away. He was tall with long legs, and I felt short in comparison at 5'2". At the end of the night, he ended up asking for my phone number.

"Sorry, I don't give out my number." I told him. "I come with my friends in the corner table every Wednesday. I'll meet you here next Wednesday. And the next time, wear a paper bag over your head. Ha ha".

We ended up dating from Fall into Spring. His name was Adam and he was from New Braunfels, Texas. During Spring Break, I took my kids to New Braunfels to check out the place. He asked me to marry him in the summer. He was going back home, and I would join him after school ended for the summer.

To pave the way for my children to join me in New Braunfels, I resigned from the El Paso School District to marry Adam. I left for New Braunfels a week early to surprise Adam.

He already had an apartment for us. I drove my car to our new apartment.

"He is going to be so surprised!" I thought.

I climbed up to the second floor where our apartment was and prepared to yell "Surprise" when he opens the door. Instead I knocked and two children came to the door. For a second I thought I was in the wrong apartment.

I asked them, "Do you know Adam?"

The boy responds, "Yes, my mom and Adam went out to rent a truck to move to Seattle. We're leaving in the morning."

I thought for a second, "But....I left my job in El Paso! I don't have a job or a place to stay!" If I had left El Paso at the agreed time, the following week, Adam would have left for Seattle and the apartment...our apartment... would have been vacant when I arrived. Adam was not going to marry... me.

I called my older daughter in San Antonio which is about 45 minutes from New Braunfels and told her the story... crying. It was summer 1991. My daughter and her husband offered me a place to stay. I would share my 3-year-old grandson's bedroom.

But before I leave New Braunfels, I am going to find Adam! went looking all over town for him. "I... don't have a job... or a place to live." Of course, I didn't find him. I would meet up with Adam several years later.

I discovered along the way that God had a plan for me... a bigger plan.

I started looking for a counseling job in San Antonio. It was summer and school districts usually start interviewing for the upcoming school year in March. Positions are filled by the end of the school year. I was offered the last counseling position in the San Antonio School District. I would stay with my daughter until I found my own apartment closer to the new school.

Two of my children were still in El Paso when I started a new school year in San Antonio. I was not married, separated from two of my children and living out of my suitcase in my grandson's bedroom. As I look back now, after 28 years of "events" I ask, "what's the lesson?"

The 1991-92 school year began and I met with the faculty and staff. Among the friends I made at this new school was a first year school teacher, Susan. The young teacher whose face I found on Facebook in October 2019. The Caucasian woman with the two Hispanic daughters. We were both new to the school district and became good friends.

In our talks, I found out that Susan was having a hard time being away from her family in Michigan for the first time. We spent a lot of time in my office at school. Susan opened up and shared some trauma that she experienced as a child. She shared some paintings she did when sad...maybe depressed. So by the end of the school year, Susan being away from family and the childhood trauma, was suicidal. We had become good friends and spent a lot of time together.

At the same time, I received information that my son that I had left in El Paso was not doing so well. I had to think of a plan to help my friend Susan and go home to my son.

"Would you go to El Paso with me?" Susan agreed to go home with me. We both resigned our positions at school at the end of the school year and stored her furniture in El Paso. Susan spent the summer with me and my two kids.

Summer of 1992 seems kind of blurred, tending to my son's problems and working with Susan's suicidal state. By the end of the summer, Susan was better and wanted to go back home to her family in Michigan. Susan was out of danger and could go on with her life.

My God has followed both of us and now 2019, He has connected our lives again through Facebook. We caught up through Facebook Messenger.

Susan had returned to Michigan and applied to 36 school districts, but they all said they could only hire her part time. This wasn't a viable option. She returned to San Antonio and was hired by Northeast ISD with one class in Special Education Adaptive Life class, the Friday prior to school starting. She then traveled to El Paso, retrieved her car and all her belongings out of storage. She then moved in with a mutual friend of ours, Judy, In San Antonio. Over the next few years the school district required her to go back to school and she completed her Master's degree in Special Education.

During this time, Susan met a man that was very abusive. She dated him for a year and became pregnant but lost the baby in a miscarriage. She once again fell into depression. Her boyfriend continued to be abusive and when he threatened her life, she got out of the relationship.

The relief she felt was not long lasting! The boyfriend started stalking Susan. Feeling lonely and missing someone to share moments with, prompts her to go back to him. Three months of marriage counseling later, Susan walks away from the abusive relationship.

Disillusioned with the end of her relationship, Susan declared, "I am not waiting for a man to have a child." She consulted with her ob/gyn, who found that her uterus had not formed properly and recommended surgery. Six months after her surgery, Susan made several attempts at artificial insemination. But these were unsuccessful and Susan began to look at adoption as a viable option.

She contacted CPS (Children Protective Services) that informed her that it was easier to qualify for adoption by being a foster home parent first. It took months of classes, inspection of her house, and many reference letters by friends before Susan was cleared as a foster to adopt home. Then came the waiting for a child. It meant Susan calling the agency every Tuesday.

In 2003, Susan received a call from a caseworker to place a baby girl detoxing from heroin with her. She was at school and ran to her principal, "If you let me go now, I could be a mom today!" The principal said, "Why are you still here?"

When she reached the hospital, the baby girl had been detoxing for 27 days. The state took custody of the baby and placed her with Susan because they were not sure the baby was going to make it. Susan fostered Jennifer (Jenny) for two years and finally got to adopt her on December 6, 2005.

During this time, Susan also served as a foster parent to other detoxing babies and kids. Susan's best friend and support system had been diagnosed with breast cancer. Susan stepped up to help care for her two daughters, a 6th grader and 3rd grader, while she underwent radiation, chemotherapy, and surgery.

Susan's friend passed away from cancer in 2006 and her girls went and lived with their grandparents away from San Antonio.

The loss of her friend, her two girls moving away with their grandparents plunged Susan back into depression. She decided to go back to Michigan with Jenny, without securing a job which led to subbing for the next seven years.

Jenny, who by this time was seven years old, started telling Susan that she wanted a sister. Susan's thoughts were that Jenny's mother could have had other children, but she was glad she hadn't brought any more babies into this world addicted to drugs.

Susan received a call one day while she was shopping at Wal-Mart with Jenny. "This is so-so with CPS in Bexar County, Texas, understand you have adopted a little girl through us before... I am calling to say we have a half-sister to your daughter and we are wondering if you would be interested in adopting her?"

Susan can't remember what she said, maybe something to the effect of "can I call you back?"

Susan just sat, getting all choked up, this DECISION would be a life changing decision.

Susan's mother strongly shut down the conversation, "Let someone else raise her!" People at church didn't get it. Her sister said, "But that is mom's house." She was living in her parents' rental property. Could she go against her mother's advice?

Susan wanted Jenny to have a "family" when she dies. Her research said that siblings have the longest relationships in life. She thought she was doing the right thing. She thought...

It was August 3, 2010 when the call came in. Susan responded with yes to adopting her, Jenny's half-sister. She had to get her home certified as a foster home again before the end of October. Then Susan could foster her. Jessie arrived on July 2, 2011, adorable but overweight.

LIFE as Susan and Jenny knew it CHANGED!

At 11 months old, Jessie knew what Cheetos and soda were. So Susan and Jenny started over with baby food. Jessie screamed for 2 weeks straight because she wanted to eat what she wanted.

It was evident that the drugs had affected Jessie considerably more than Jenny. She would grab food from the plates of anyone near her. She would make herself throw up at the table. She refused to follow directions.

Life HAD changed, sadly between the age of 2 and 4, Susan was seriously considering dissolving the adoption. Medication made things better but Jenny's ANGER never rests!

Jessie was impulsive, hyperactive, and lacked the ability to self-regulate her anger. All these behaviors were confirmed by professionals at the age of five.

Susan was finally able to buy a house for the three of them in 2014.

Six years later, now, Jenny lives with depression and anxiety, this is said to be affected by her biological mother's drug use. She is also dyslexic. Even through her struggles, she has remained tough. At 16, she wants to be a special education teacher, learn to drive, and be rich.

Jessie is now nine and continues to struggle with her impulsiveness and anger issues but is compassionate and sees the good in others. She does well in school. She loves puzzles and boys! She recently said, "Mom, I want to be like you! Be a teacher, with no man, drinking iced tea."

Susan had lived with the dream of having a family of her own. Twenty-eight years of serving God and several communities across the country, she finally has her own home and two daughters. The two girls have found themselves hundreds of miles away from their birthplace, with a loving mother and unconditional love in a forever home. Who but God could bring all people together through TIME AND SPACE!

"Every moment of every day, what you feel in your heart is a command in the Mind of God. The Mind of God interprets our feelings very, very literally." - Gregg Braden

WE'RE ALL IN THIS TOGETHER

"God is our refuge and strength, a very present help in trouble."
Psalm 46

I'm a Licensed Professional Counselor and have been in practice for 30 years. I was divorced 40 years ago. I am writing my third book, which will hopefully be published in the next 6 months.

This book is literally how God has guided me through my life to serve people. This book contains ten or more stories on how God's Plan for each of us connects people in all walks of life to bring this about.

I have come to the major story of my life…my divorce. The Plan that God set in motion 55 years ago. I was married in 1963 and divorced in 1979. I cannot say that I didn't give the marriage enough time to work. I had finished high school, was married and when my two daughters started school, I went back to school to become a teacher. The last year of my bachelors, I ended up pregnant with my son, and still walking up and down the hills of the UTEP campus.

I had just gone through another scary Friday night. My husband's Friday night out ended up quite late, while I worked on my homework. I sat on our recliner in the middle of the living room where I could see the back door, the front door and the hallway where our children slept. I was afraid to be alone in the house. I would wait to go to bed, until he came home.

Next morning, I was up early because my husband had a part time job on Saturdays. I would do the wash early. While emptying the pockets of the pants that he wore last night, I found evidence of his unfaithfulness! I was crying and thinking…." what do I do now.... this is the end of my marriage! I need a nightlight to sleep... how do I go on? My two little girls...my son!"

A car door slammed outside! My husband had remembered what was in his pants pocket and was rushing back! All I did was turn around with my hands behind me! Of course, he took the evidence back and was out the rest of the day.

Now 30 years of private practice, I am faced with working on my main story for this book. My publisher and I talked about the divorce story! "No! No! I don't want to write the divorce story! I cried. It's an ugly story!"

I wrote the divorce story.

My publisher read it. "If this is a book on God in your life, where is God in this story...

A split second, I was crying..." He wasn't there! He abandoned me for fourteen years!" I was shocked as the words came out of my mouth!

And for 40 years when I hear from my clients in the office, "God, God why have you forsaken me?" I am there as a therapist to reaffirm the client that God is our protector, the world is the world, all kinds of ugly things happen in this world, but God comforts and protects. God doesn't punish. Ugly things don't happen because we have sinned or broken the commandments. I closed my ears to myself saying, "God, why have you forsaken me?" So, two days ago, I broke my 40 years of silence, in my fourteen year marriage for me and my children.

I walked away from that marriage with my children and never looked back.

In my personal life, I'm trying to rewrite the divorce story. And it started with what I had released from deep in my being. Somewhere in my mind, I had not seen God protecting me all along the 14 years I was married.

"God...God was not there," I blurted out with a burst of tears.

Yet my children and I have been well. "For I know the plans I have for you," declares the Lord, "plans to prosper you and not to harm you, plans to give you hope and a future." Jeremiah 29:11

God's plan included working on the thought that had been buried deep in my heart. I had not cleared my heart. But for the grace of God, my children and I were healthy and well educated. We had faith in the same God to build **a future for ourselves.**

And this year, God's plan, through time and space **to give you hope and a future** has reached me. I have met through my private practice two young women. Both women in their forties, with a marriage of many years, a child or two, abuse and a man with no mercy. Both women are going through court on custody issues. God has connected me with these women who are experiencing the same issues I had gone through forty years ago.

The God I know, used my fourteen years of marriage to help these women, knowing well the feelings they were experiencing. Calling on God to comfort these women and calling on those women to trust God, when they release those children to their birth fathers. God never leaves them alone, He protects them, and He brings them back home.

The first woman that I will call, Linda, lives here in San Antonio. She has a 5-year-old girl; Jan. Linda was married for 7 years. Her husband was an alcoholic and abusive when drunk. When she was six months pregnant, her husband Mike became even more abusive, almost targeting the yet unborn child. He didn't want to share Linda with the baby. He was seeing another woman when the baby was born. Eventually Linda divorced Mike and made a life of her own with her little girl. He married the woman he had been seeing when Linda was pregnant.

Linda's life changed a couple of years later. She met Ben. Ben was the opposite of Mike. He was kind, patient and loved Linda's little girl. The setting in this relationship was quite different. Linda learned about love and trust with Ben. Her little girl felt loved and cherished. Ben introduced Jan to horses, walks and spent time with her. It took time for Linda to learn to trust again. After some time, Linda married Ben and they became a family, a happy family. She has many videos in her iPhone of the happy times the three shared. Jan is always asking to see the videos.

One day, Linda was at work when she received a phone call. Ben had been working outdoors when a swarm of bees attacked him! He died later in the hospital.

That same day I was ready to leave the office when I received a call for an appointment. It sounded urgent. I asked the woman to come right over to my office.

The session was very emotional! Linda was still in shock, having just identified her husband's body. While Linda was at the hospital, her in-laws had gone into their home, and had taken everything! She didn't know what to do!

Ben and Linda had just married less than a month before and Ben's family went into their apartment and took everything.

Linda didn't return. I didn't see her again for eighteen months. Many times, I wondered what had happened to her.

She called this year to make an appointment for herself and her six-year-old. Because of COVID 19, I worked with Linda through telehealth. She was preparing for another round in court with her ex-husband on his visitation.

Linda was angry! She was protecting her child! She felt that visitation for three days, five hours away was not safe. She was in the bathroom on a telehealth session with me. Her fear of allowing her daughter to a place away from her was too much.

Yet Linda could not break down with her daughter in the next room doing school on the computer. During our fourth session, she reported having terrible nightmares. It hurt me just to watch her anger take over her and sobbing all through the therapy session.

I invited Linda to come to a second session that same week. There was more relief for her using EMDR in the office. She worked hard in session, and she had a breakthrough her anger.

As I worked with her, the same kind of pictures and feelings played in the back of my mind. A week after Linda's session with EMDR, her nightmares stopped. She reported feeling a shift in her anger that was causing her nightmares.

Linda brings her little girl to play therapy in the afternoons. Through Jan's drawings and laughing through the videos of the happy moments she experienced with Ben, both mother and daughter talked about how they miss him so much! Then once they get home Jan cries more. Linda was able to grieve for her husband alongside her daughter.

Linda's move from her anger to grieving helped her express herself the next week when she went back to court on the custody case. The mediation session on visitation was hard on Linda and Jan.

The temporary orders stated that Jan was to go visit her father for 10 days for Christmas break. She struggled to release her six-year-old to her father for 10 days 5 hours away. The heartless man had done away with Linda's morning call to her daughter. The new temporary orders still left a call to Jan from Linda at night. Both mother and daughter felt the impact.

Linda took care of that by scheduling herself at work for extra shifts....to keep busy.

In the same couple of months, the second woman on my schedule was Karla, a young woman in her 40's, two children and an abusive husband. God arranged these two women to me a therapist that had run off after her divorce.

I had locked away all those feelings in a closet with a black door. Forty years had gone by, and the door was suddenly swung open by two identical cases scheduled weekly side by side, Wednesday morning and Thursday morning.

"Timing is not ours; God calls the time." My belief.

Karla's abusive marriage of 12 years and 2 children, 10 and 7 became too much for a woman with Lupus and a kidney transplant.

The stress from her drunk husband's abuse resulted in the transplant failing.

Karla picked up her two children and left her husband. Her mother passed away around this time and Karla found herself and her children living in a friend's parent's basement in Pittsburg. The Pandemic helped in that her children were being schooled online.

Karla's improving her situation for herself, and her children included sending a letter to the new medical center in a new state to consider getting her on a new list for a new kidney.

Karla now has a home of her own and the medical center has removed the failed kidney. New friends have tended to her children while she had her surgery.

Karla had a college friend in Texas that was a client of mine. My client introduced me to Karla and she became my client. **God working again through time and space.** The two women had kept in touch for years. I had worked with my client a year earlier on her divorce.

For weeks my therapeutic relationship with each of these women had consisted of descriptive scenes of physical and verbal abuse, protecting children, and financial hardships. The reflective paraphrasing, while working with these two women, seemed to have shifted what had been stored away for 40 years in my closet.

God had been with me during the 14 years of my marriage, kept me and my children safe. God knows each of us by name and has a plan for us.

THE WILDERNESS

My time in the wilderness was the fourteen years that I lost early in my life. If I may compare the danger of wild animals and things in the dark, to angry people and explosive tempers that go off, it was so.

The week before, riding in the car with my husband, on the highest loop on the freeway in town, I heard, "The next time I will just go straight."

That was God's message if I ever heard one. My God has kept my children and myself safe all our lives.

God led me out of the wilderness, so I thought. When my husband was slashing the couches with a knife, I grabbed my three kids and ran next door to a neighbor's house to call my father. He picked us up and asked, "Shall I take you to the justice of the peace?"

At that time, that was where you file for a divorce.

My father was a quiet man but had witnessed what was going on for many years. He didn't interfere , but his suggestion spoke volumes to me.

For the next month, my father would drive us to our house, where we would sit in his car and wait for my husband to leave for work. The kids and I would go in and get clothes for school while my father kept an eye out for my husband. If my father yelled, "I see the truck …". We would run out and leave.

It was a month before the court hearing, where the judge asked my husband to move out, so that kids and I could come back home.

My first month back, my daughter Liz went out back to throw out the trash. She came in all excited…she found a litter of freshly born mice! How does one get rid of mice?

Call grandpa, my father. Grandpa was busy for the next ten years. He fixed flat tires, cleaned the swamp coolers that are used in El Paso, and wouldn't let me take my children to Disneyland without him and my mother.

My kids and I all slept in the same bed for a while and slowly we went back to our own bedrooms. We began our lives back to normalcy. That included the back of a chair under the doorknob of the two doors to the outside. That was the first alarm to keep my children safe. My nightlight was on at the end of the day.

Every day I went to work, after leaving the girls at school and my little four-year-old at my mother's house. The girls would walk back home and became "latch key" kids. They would call my mother, letting her know they were home. I would pick up the girls after work, drop them at my mother's and go on to evening classes at UT El Paso. I was determined to become a teacher. My parents and five sisters worked together as my support system.

At times several families would get together and go camping in Ruidoso, New Mexico and of course, mom and dad were included. My brothers-in-law each bought a pickup truck to go camping. I had to have a pickup with a camper shell to take my kids camping. Families that camp together stay together.

One evening we were all sitting around the campfire when we hear lots of yelling! My father had gone to the bathrooms around the campgrounds and a bear was chasing him! Of course, with all the noise from the family, the bear ran off.

So, my children and I were always around family. My uncle introduced me to one of his friends in the military. He was also into camping. Weeks later, Tony met my family on a Sunday.

Every Sunday was my Mother's Day. All six of us girls would go to church with our own families and then meet at grandma's. We would have lunch together and the cousins would play. Sunday routine was the same as forever.

My sisters were in the kitchen getting lunch ready with mom.

I would join the men playing cards with my father. I learned how to play 31, poker, and blackjack. My father taught me to shuffle. I invited Tony, now boyfriend, on Sunday.

I was with the group of men at the card table shuffling, when Tony quietly pulled me aside.

Tony softly asked me, "Shouldn't you be in the kitchen with the women?"

I was shocked...my brothers-in-law never...refused to play with me. Later I realized Tony is Hispanic and 10 years older than me! So, I got up and went into the kitchen with my sisters and mother.

As one of my poems in my book goes:

> My Self Esteem
> My self-esteem was at its peak,
> My head held high,
> My spirits flew,
> I finally knew what I could.
>
> My name spelled all that
> Life had to offer.
> My dreams soared high
> And I felt fine.
>
> How could I fail?
> How could I fall?
> It took a Macho
> With hands on hips,
> To let me know
> What I had failed to comprehend.
>
> All that I had,
> It took a man
> A whole lifetime to have and attain.
>
> It was unforgivable.
> It was unheard,
> To see a woman that had so much.

GOD IS MY BOSS

In my office, being a Licensed Professional Counselor for thirty years, I pride myself in keeping up with new training. In my practice, I am self-confident and self-assured. I have new clients come into my office every week, while other clients have been with me through a couple of generations. I am serving their children or grandchildren. I work with children, adults and families. I am fully aware that I serve God and his children, whatever age. By now, I can tell when God has sent someone to my door.

Sometimes I find a plain piece of paper taped to my door in Spanish or I arrive at work to find the whole family in the waiting room ready to make an appointment. There is always an urgency in their voice that I hear.

I figured out a few years ago the office was not my office. God has been running my business for HIS people. When my humanness gets in His way and by accident, I schedule two persons for the same time, God has one of the clients call and cancel, to correct my mistake.

God is a great Provider so that I can work free (Pro Bono) as needed. My time is God's to arrange and rearrange sessions. At times gas money appears to make sure that the family makes it to therapy. Sometimes I go home early but most of the time I get home late.

A few years ago, my Ego was getting in the way.

God had educated me and led me to all kinds of training to be able to work with children through Play Therapy and EMDR (Eye Movement Desensitization Reprocessing) for adults, Biomagnetism, REIKI and Bioenergetic for all ages.

My Ego always said, "Good job, Trini!"

Even though at times I would be puzzled. What had worked so well, wasn't in my repertoire of classes or words that I knew. God was ahead of me in "knowing" what was needed to heal the person or the family.

When a woman called after 8:00 at night, because she needed to talk to someone right after she was told her husband was dying. Once he was declared dead, her husband's family had run to their house and ransacked the house and took everything. She needed a session so she could vent and cry with someone over her loss and strategize how to get her things back, before picking up her five-year-old daughter. She needed support to calm down and not scare her child.

Another case was to evaluate a young woman named Betty in college to find a way to avoid getting legal charges brought against her.

She had been raised on a secluded large ranch and was homeschooled through high school. When she started college, what she didn't learn in high school about trust got her in legal trouble. Betty shared a room with another girl and became friends with her. When her roommate found a boyfriend, all three ended up having the same major in college. They attended the same classes and part of their internship was at NASA in the space program. The couple decided to steal the moon rocks brought back from the moon that were on display.

Betty didn't know their plans to steal the rocks. They asked her for a ride to NASA to pick up an assignment. Betty had a car and drove the couple to NASA. She waited in the car for them. Once inside they couldn't open the display box with the rocks, so they ran outside with the whole box. And Betty, not knowing what they had done, drove them back to the dorm. The couple was not caught until they tried to sell the "moon rocks" on the internet. And all three were arrested. Betty was charged as an accomplice.

The social assessment for Betty's defense showed that since she had been isolated and homeschooled, Betty was lacking the social skills for interacting with others out in the real world. She didn't learn the social skills of trust. High school experiences with other teenagers develop a very important instinct as to friends and trust. She had driven the car when the couple stole the moon rocks at NASA. The assessment report proved that. Betty's charges, as an accomplice were dropped. After our last session, Betty left the office with the report for her lawyer, and I was alone in the building.

This is when I ended up feeling pretty smart, and adding "Good Job, Trini" as I walked to the back of my empty office.

I believe God had run out of patience with me.

Out from the back of the building at the end of the hall I heard, a **BOOMING VOICE** say,

"YOUR GOD IS A LOVING GOD, BUT HE IS ALSO A JEALOUS GOD!"

That voice put me in my place! I hadn't done the work. God had!

Since then, people ask me how I can deal with all these clients and their situations. I say,

I DON'T DO THE WORK, GOD DOES. NO BOOMING VOICE FOR ME AGAIN.

ONCE I WAS BLIND BUT NOW...

I lost 14 years in my twenties. Those years include memories of my babies, their first tooth, their first steps, and their first words. My memory is triggered by photos, and I occasionally take out boxes of pictures and relive that time.

These years of marriage to my husband have been blocked forever by my brain. We married very young, two strong willed individuals with nothing in common but wanting to be free adults. It became a power struggle. Those years were ugly. The brain is a marvelous thing, protecting us from what is too painful to remember. While I am glad, I don't remember the marriage, I have often mourned the loss of these years and memories in my family's life.

"God, You are so good to me!"

In 2020, the pandemic happened! Only God would use the Pandemic for something positive. It has been a year of loss and devastation for the world . . .

And 2020 started that way for my family: my children, my grandchildren, and my great-grandchildren. Every adult in my family ended up working from home. We started getting together at my daughter Liz's new home that she shares with her significant other, Joe. My older daughter Betty, son Raul and Alexis, and my stepson Sully. They would at times invite friends from work, Joes' sister and her husband and my granddaughter, Alyssa and her husband Nate would also join us. The great-grandchildren didn't come very often, so it was mainly a houseful of young adults. This grew into a large group that was and is meeting twice a month for birthdays. Everyone kept with the pandemic rules to keep the group safe.

At first, the group came up with some drinking games for the evening. That made me uncomfortable, so I invited my Lord to the group. I added the group to my church's prayer list and the most amazing thing happened!

The group shifted focus to food and ended up with at least 10 chefs. Twice a month we celebrated birthdays and Liz, and Joe's big kitchen is full of chefs in every corner. The theme for the evening has been decided the meeting before: seafood, Mexican, Italian, French, or appetizers.

Each chef is given a number instead of their name for the judges. There are points for presentation of their entry, color scheme, and taste. Betty, my daughter, bought a wooden cooking spoon, sprayed it with gold, and VOLA!.. . a trophy! This agenda has been followed for the course of the pandemic.

This bi-monthly meeting of my family has deeply touched me. The loss of 14 years, memories when they were growing up, has been replaced with these memories and interactions of these last 10 months.

My children, friends, and significant others greeting each other, laughing, and teasing each other makes the pandemic appear far faraway.

I walk in early or at least on time to enjoy their entrance. I sit around the kitchen counter so I can view the backdoor, and when it opens, I am ready for the hugs and laughter that follows.

Raul, my son, and Alexis come in pulling their wagon full of food ingredients for their two entries in the cooking contest. My daughter, Betty, comes in with her big dog. Others come in at their own pace.

Another round of greetings, laughter, and catching up. I sit there just taking in the generous portions of love being passed around.

On New Year's, a long table was set up for all the grown-ups and a small table for the great-grandchildren. Each one listed what they accomplished in 2020, followed by their new year's resolution.

Mine was obvious, "God, You are so good to me!"

I intentionally move one step back as a mom, "Lord, these are good people!"

GOD'S AT WORK AND DOING WELL

It was 2004 when I met Anthony and his sister. Anthony was 4 and in Pre-K. He and his sister who is older by a couple of years had been adopted by a distant family member. Being a child therapist, I worked with both children for a few years. As time went on, the adoptive mother also brought her grandchildren to my office. As the years passed, she would call for advice, until Anthony grew up and finished high school. His mother would keep me on top of the activities that Anthony was involved in.

Several years ago, I learned that Anthony ran away from home. He went to live with an aunt and then with his sister. Anthony was smoking pot. He was homeless for some months.

Finally, Anthony came back home to his adoptive mother and father. Rules were set for him. He had a job, and he was paying his parents rent. Counseling was brought up and an appointment was made. Mother and father had a plan for the three to meet with me.

When Tuesday's appointment came, Anthony came into the office by himself. Mother and father sat outside in the truck watching him walk in. I had all the background information on Anthony's drug problem. I had no idea how to get Anthony to talk about his drug problem.

I met Anthony at the door and walked him to my office. I hadn't seen him in a couple of years. I asked him, "how old are you...what have you been doing?"

Anthony told me about finishing school and has a great job. It would be the perfect job if it wasn't for a coworker that isn't nice to him. Anthony kept talking about the coworker and getting upset, the more he talked about her.

It was then that I invited God into the session. Anthony went on telling me about his boss. As he talked about his boss, the energy in the room grew. His boss has been teaching him how to invest in stocks. He was proud of himself for investing! He took out his iPhone and showed me the screen that showed his profits of $122.00!

Anthony's enthusiasm was filling up the whole office! It was contagious! God had led me to Anthony's secret key to do God's work. "Anthony, who is big enough to get you a job with a boss that is willing to teach you a new way of life, GOD! "Anthony had been an altar boy when he was younger. He believes in God.

I asked him if he was setting up another appointment. I said, "I have a sliding scale in paying for the next appointment… is $40.00 ok with you? "Yes," said Anthony.

Not only is Anthony setting up another appointment, but he is paying for it!

But the surprise came after Anthony walked out of my office. He was walking out of my office when his parents were waiting in the truck for him. His mother was texting me, "what happened? My husband saw Anthony walk into the building and it wasn't the same Anthony coming out, full of confidence and happiness!"

"God joined our session!"

Therapy sessions lasted a year. Anthony would get up early on his only day off, to come to session.

DANIEL

There is a huge yellow house that was ready to fall and had been built in the 1920s. This house was situated across from my office that my client, Amanda, lived in while she was working on her degree. I had met Amanda in 2014, and she was the friendliest person I knew. Amanda was in her thirties and very down to earth, she came in once a week, very consistently, for sessions, and she worked on her familial relationships. During her time with me, she would come in, take off her shoes, and lay on the floor. This was her time for herself.

When she would take a break from her studies, she would routinely go jogging down to the river or street. She would often tell me about the people she had met on these outings. She made friends with these people and would listen to their stories. Then she would stay connected with them, checking on them daily.

During the two years she was my patient, she talked about a man that lived down the street across from the taco lady. She would stop in to check on him on her walks, or he would bring her fruit and candy. They became good friends. She also talked about a retired older gentleman who she would bring cookies and play with his dog.

After some time, she decided to go back home to finish her degree in social work. I missed her when she left. We would text back and forth for a while.

She would often ask me about the man that lived across from the taco lady. I had made time to identify the house that I passed on my way to and from my office every day. But I never saw anyone outside.

One day as I passed the house an ambulance was sitting outside. I texted Amanda to let her know since, I had never met him.

Later I found out that he had been ready to commit suicide while drinking. He had put a sharp knife on the table in his living room, scared himself, and called 911.

The dispatcher had sent a police car and an ambulance. The police were quite familiar with his number.

About a month later, I was at the mailboxes for my office, when a man in his forties came up to me. He looked like a giant to me. He must have been 6'5" and wore a cowboy hat and boots. He had one of my business cards in his hand, dirty and kind of worn out.

"Do you know Amanda?" He inquired as he slurred his words.

I had to think a second, "Yes."

"Amanda gave me your business card. I have carried it with me for two years. I need your help." I walked him into my office and that was my first session with Amanda's friend, Daniel, who lived across from the taco lady.

Daniel was finally grieving the loss of his family; he was the last one. He had neglected his family during his last 15-20 years with drugs.

He missed his mother who adored him and spoiled him all his life. Daniel believed that he could not go visit his mother's grave drunk because she didn't want him drinking.

After his first visit, Daniel left my office and said that he would not have been able to come to my office without a couple of drinks.

I set a hard rule for Daniel. I told him, He could not come to a session when drunk. There were times when he would cancel the session and truthfully state that he had been drinking all night, "and you told me that I have to be sober to come to the session."

Another time, Daniel showed up drunk to his session. I picked up the keys next to him and offered to take him home until he sobered up. I dropped him at his home and left the keys with him.

The truck was still in my parking lot when I went home at the end of the day.

At the beginning, Daniel was always saying that he wanted to die, "I don't want to live." He had inherited the language and suicidal ideation from his uncle, who had committed suicide in the very house that Daniel was living in.

At that time, he was looking for a job. Daniel owned the house where he lived but didn't have the money to pay taxes owed or utilities. His body was not in the best of health after 20 years of abusing it. He stated that he had experience painting houses. His friends would at times hire him to help them paint a house or two.

I worked with Daniel that summer. He would get drunk, think of suicide, find a knife, scared himself, and now would call me.

One day, the call came as I was driving to church. All summer I witnessed the police picking Daniel up after such a call, dry him up overnight and release him 24 hours later.

I drove away from church and drove to the police department. No one was there on Sunday, so I had the attention of the skeleton staff. I went over my observations of the whole summer and I said, "then you throw him back out there. Do something! I am his therapist." Well, the police did do something.

Daniel ended up in Kerrville Rehab. He was very upset with me. Well, very angry.

"I don't want to hear the word suicide again." I told him. And I haven't… heard it.

At therapy, I gave him homework. If he was grieving, he was to write about his family.

Daniel turned out to be a terrific poet. He would read the poem and we would work on the feelings within the poem. I would give him a twenty-dollar bill and make him a copy of his poem. That became a part of his therapy for the next two years.

He began to add art to his daily activities.

In 2020, Daniel decided to sell his home. He sold it just before the county would claim it. The last six months, Daniel found that painting on paper calms him down. He has used some of his house money for art materials.

I don't buy his poems anymore. Daniel says, "These are free."

He is now on a very strict budget. So, the sessions switched over to budgeting and getting a job.

I have worked with Daniel for two years. Recently, he asked me to go to the cemetery with him, "My Mom wants to meet you."

What I experienced was this 6"5' little boy crying as he introduced me to his mother and left us alone to talk. The little boy offered some advice as he walked away from the gravesite, "It's going to sound like someone whispering in your ear."

God's greatest commandment is…" love thy neighbor as thyself." Amanda still checks on Daniel. At least Daniel has adopted the sober rule to visit his mother's gravesite.

What I have learned about Daniel the last two years is that he knows… knows the bible all the way through. Somewhere he also has read a lot about angels. He has a vast wealth of knowledge.

In his free time, which is all day, he has visited different church groups and different AA groups. He was down to two beers a day until he went on a binge, and during that time, he met a young woman in her thirties and her significant other. They met while drinking and still drink together. Daniel shared that she has been drinking for a long time like him.

But God's plan steps in. It was Veteran's Day and the man being a veteran drank too much. He started being abusive to his girlfriend. The couple was from out of town and ran out of money so Daniel paid for a room for them for several days. After some point, the abusive man left town abandoning the woman.

Two days later, Daniel comes to me crying. The young woman's father is military, and his helicopter has just been shot down in Kuwait. She must leave town to go see her father. Her mother is meeting her in Houston to go to the hospital. Daniel calls, "Trini, let's pray for her father, he is on a respirator, and they have to decide when to turn it off."

To date, that is the longest prayer I have ever prayed.

A couple of weeks later, the young woman, Stephanie, came back to town and met up with Daniel. They end up talking a lot and becoming friends. In those conversations they share their thoughts on alcohol. How long they both have been drinking and they form a plan to cut down and detox. The relationship gets serious, and Stephanie becomes Daniel's girlfriend. They are putting their resources together to find a place to live. Daniel continues to keep me informed on their life.

"Faith, hope and love, these three, but the greatest of these is love"

1 Corinthians 13:13

TWENTY DOLLAR BILLS

Philippians 4:19 And my God will meet all your needs according to his glorious riches in Christ Jesus.

I became a single mom of 3 at age 35. My two girls were 13 and 10, and my son was four years old. My son, who is now 47, grew up with the concept of a living God. He believes in a God that is always here to provide for our needs.

I raised my three children in El Paso, Texas, and moved to San Antonio, Texas away from my support system about 3 years after my divorce. I worked on a budget with figures that included my salary from the San Antonio School District, deductions for the Texas Teacher Retirement, rent for an apartment big enough for a single mom, two teenage girls and a 7-year-old boy, plus food.

Living without my support group was a rough time for me. I knew things would be a little tight with the budget, but no one would starve. When I started working and got my first paycheck, I realized that San Antonio, unlike my school district in El Paso, took out both Texas Teacher Retirement and Social Security. I was devastated because the difference in money left us without money for food.

My two girls had started working at local food restaurants. Betty worked the late shift at McDonalds and would bring home hamburgers that would normally be thrown away at the end of the day.

Liz was working the late shift at One Potato Two and she would bring home potatoes that would typically be thrown away at the end of the day. That summer we ate a lot of late dinners.

I only got paid once a month so on the third Friday of the month, I would be short on resources and big on needs.

"God, you gave me three children. I just need a little help. Just $20 more would do it." I would go into the shower, cry, pray, and call out to God. "If I could just have $20 for milk and bread. I get paid next week and then everything will be good."

I didn't want to scare the kids, so I would wipe away any trace of tears. During these tough times, my kids and I lost count of how many times Raul found a $20 bill somewhere. We would be on our way to soccer practice and there would be a $20 bill in the bush, on the street, or he would find one in a dirty pair of jeans. The next time he would find one on the baseball field or in our backyard. We never knew where one would pop up, but it was during this time of random $20 bills that we made ends meet.

These $20 bills were more than just a loaf of bread or a gallon of milk to us. They were evidence that God was with us during this time of need in our family. When we found $20, we knew that we were not alone in this struggle even with my parents, our support system so far away.

The $20 bills were not the only example we had during this time of God providing for our needs.

One time our car broke down and our neighbor just happened to know how to fix it. God also found us a place that would only open after midnight to buy groceries and would allow us to buy more food for our money. Someone called it the black market. It was these moments that we knew that God was in control, and we would not starve. This impacted all of us on a deep level and set a foundation for my children's faith. Now at 47, my son believes that his God will provide for him, his sisters, and that everything he needs is right within his reach.

MY CAR WON'T GO HOME

"For I know the plans I have for you," declares the Lord, "plans to prosper you and not to harm you, plans to give you hope and a future. 12 Then you will call on me and come and pray to me, and I will listen to you. 13 You will seek me and find me when you seek me with all your heart. 14 I will be found by you," declares the Lord, "and will bring you back from captivity. I will gather you from all the nations and places where I have banished you," declares the Lord, "and will bring you back to the place from which I carried you into exile." Jeremiah 29:11-14

As an elementary school counselor, I had been working on a program for At Risk Children. These students between the ages of 5 and 11 were having school problems, lacking social skills, and needed strong authority figures in their life.

I was putting together a plan to find mentors in the Hispanic community for each of them, such as the neighborhood store owner, the local sheriff, and the McDonald's manager. I was also scheduling mini workshops with parents on discipline and communication skills with their children. These workshops had meant extending my days at school, and this day had been one of the long ones.

It was 8:00 at night and my feet were killing me. I had been on my feet for 12 hours, and I was ready to go home when I backed out of the parking lot and turned my car towards home.

Suddenly I began to panic, my car wasn't turning towards it and was going in the opposite direction.

"God, why now? I'm tired and I just want to go home." My car was taken over and I got to an intersection. "Time to get back on route." I thought, but instead of turning again towards home, my car went crazy and took another wrong turn, and then another.

"God, not today! What could be so important that it has to be taken care of at 8:00 at night?" There was no answer. I had had enough experience, that faith began to take over and I let God drive.

Of course, my hands are on the steering wheel. This is not my route home. Twenty minutes later, still holding onto the wheel, I end up at the mall. But not the mall that is closest to my house. By this point it is close to 9 pm and the mall is getting ready to close.

"Okay, what now? What am I looking for?" I park my car and get out. I am looking for something out of place. Something unusual.

"What am I looking for?" I ask God again. "I need a clue." The mall was almost empty, and I began by walking down the first floor. Workers are starting to clean up and getting ready to close shop.

I walk from one end of the first floor to the other end. Nothing seems unusual or out of place.

I go up the second floor and it is just as empty.

"God, I am still not seeing what you want me to." I walk again from one end of the second floor to the other and I notice a woman sitting on a bench in the mall. I thought this was unusual because everyone was getting ready to leave. But this woman seemed in no hurry to go anywhere.

As I approached her, I noticed something else about her. I knew her. She looked familiar and it finally clicked that her name was Melinda, and she was one of my friends from high school.

Immediately a knowing settled over me. This Is What God was leading me to.

I haven't seen her in 20 years.

"Melinda, it has been such a long time since I've seen you." As I greet her, I see how upset she is. "What are you doing here all alone in the middle of the mall? It is getting late."

I notice that she has been crying and as we talk, she breaks down revealing that she has been having a hard time since her divorce. She has been contemplating suicide.

She was having issues with Agoraphobia and was struggling with simple tasks such as going to the store and buying food. We began to work together to address her fears. She was able to recover.

This was a moment that I learned that God was in control, and I needed to walk on faith and trust even when I was tired. My feet hurt and I just wanted to go home. This was the meeting of another divine appointment and the impact that God had in my life.

I AM THE BELL

My friend, Roger Smith, told me the story of a blind horse and a goat. The farmer loved the horse even though he was old and blind and refused to put him down. The farmer had a goat and he placed a bell around the goat's neck. He was determined to let the old horse live out the rest of his life in the back pasture with the goat. When it was time to go in the barn each night, the horse would hear the goat's bell and follow.

My friend Roger was very special to me. I had met him in 1995 when I had moved to San Marcos, and I was working as a counselor for San Marcos CISD. Roger's parents had passed several years before. Because of this he had made his coworkers at the school his family.

I rented my front house to him at my ranch, and he became close with my family, often joining us for dinner and making desserts for us. Roger drove his noisy motorcycle up the driveway and my grandchildren would come out of the house, yelling, asking him for rides. He eventually bought his own house, not too far from the ranch.

All second-grade students wanted to be in Mr. Smith's class. He had a large aquarium with a large snake in it. Next to the aquarium was a smaller one where he was breeding mice, to feed the snake. He was always working on some project with his students, like looking for tarantulas! Roger could be found walking with his class around the campus. Parents were constantly requesting the principal to place their children in his classroom, especially the more active boys.

After school on Fridays, Roger led the group of teachers and teacher assistants to the Green Parrot Lounge in downtown San

Marcos. He was the center of the social group at school and often had friends over.

One day, US Marshals showed up at Roger's house and arrested him for some crimes on the internet. I couldn't figure out the jargon on the charges against him, but I offered to put up the bail for him. My daughter wouldn't allow me to do it, because of the nature of Roger's charges. He was too much of a risk of running because he had no family.

Roger didn't get to come back home. He was tried and convicted to 10 years in prison. One of his friends and I went and packed up his home and sold all his belongings. That money and what the school district owed him went to his bank account. I stepped in as his surrogate mother at this time and my name was added to his bank account to manage his money. He used some of that money to pay his tuition for another master's in theology during the 10 years. Roger's plan was to teach in Seminary School when his time was done.

Being a middle-class working teacher, he didn't adjust to life in prison well. Because it was a federal crime, he was eventually moved to North Carolina. He was able to correspond with several of his school friends. He would write some angry letters.

In one letter he described an incident at the prison. "Somebody started a fight, and I ended up in the middle of it, all beat up. I was in the infirmary for several days." Other times, Roger would call very depressed, informing me that the prison psychiatrist had put him on medication, and he had started going to therapy.

I received lots of letters and phone calls during those ten years. He complained that his block's AC was lowered, and he was freezing in the summer, the heater wasn't turned on and it was too cold in the winter. I would call the prison to complain about the conditions Roger was being kept in.

Roger would call me once a week from prison. He'd ask for some of his money to get food that he liked. "My celly ate all the food I bought." he would tell me. Roger ended up on antidepressants and became a very angry man. Some of his friends would write to him.

A woman named Lucy that had had her son in Roger's class wrote to him most of the ten years. They became very close. She was there encouraging him throughout the ten years until his time served was up. One of the teacher assistants and five other good friends kept in touch with him and wrote Roger for ten years.

September 2005, I went to pick Roger up from a Halfway House in San Antonio. I had retired from the schools and had a private practice in San Marcos. We went to the bank to sign his money account back to him. He couldn't drive because he didn't have a car and his driver's license had expired and he had to pass his driving test again.

Roger and I drove down IH 35 to find him a room to stay. During this process, I would drive, stop at a motel and he would go in. I stayed in the car. He would ask the motel manager to let him try the bed in the room before he paid for it. We drove through several motels, Roger trying out the beds, before he decided which room, he would stay in. My heart just broke to see the urgency on Roger's part to find a good mattress.

He eventually took his driving test and with the ten years of interest on his money he had enough money to buy a nice car, an SUV.

Then Roger went looking for an apartment. He had to reveal that he had been in prison to the landlord and not everyone wanted to rent to ex-convicts. Roger went looking for a job. He received the same dismal answer wherever he went. He visited his friends. They had jobs and so he spent a lot of time alone.

His nest egg was quickly going down. We'd have lunch together once a week.

At the end of December 2005, we talked about the future. Because of the nature of his crime I was limited in the help I could give him because I have several state licenses and it would be unethical, being a dual relationship.

One day in January 2006, Roger called to have lunch. He had invited me and some of his friends from school. It happened that I had another appointment that day. On that day, he went by my office, but I was out, so he went on his way without calling me. But he had a schedule to keep and a letter to mail,

Next day, I received a call from the New Braunfels Police Department. Roger had shot himself in a motel there. The same day I found a letter from Roger in my mailbox. The letter had his last requests:

"Trini, thank you for all you have done for me. I have asked for God's forgiveness. In a few days, Thompson Funeral Home will call you to pick up my ashes."

Roger had sold his big SUV, paid for his cremation, bought a gun, rented a motel room and shot himself.

Roger had never forgotten Lucy and her little boy that he had taught in Second grade ten years earlier. Roger had washed all the sheets in his bedroom and all his clothes. The sheets and bed would go to Lucy. Roger's clothes would go to the little boy, who was now Roger's size. The letter I had received also listed all his furniture that would go to Lucy.

He also thought about me. He rented a motel room because I would be the one cleaning up his apartment, and he didn't want me to have to clean up the crime scene.

Lucy and I met for the first-time face to face sharing the grief for OUR friend. We emptied and cleaned Roger's apartment and moved everything to Lucy's home.

When the call came from the funeral home to pick up Roger's ashes, I asked a friend of his to pick them up. His friend picked up Roger's ashes in January 2006, where they remain until now October 2020. That I could not do.

My time as Roger's bell had come to an end. My God. who knows all things, had found a friend for Roger for his last days on earth. All my life when confronted by situations too complicated for mortal man to understand, all I can say is "what's the lesson here?" Trust in the Lord, the lesson is connected to another soul.

IF I WAS A FLY ON THE WALL

Exalted to the right hand of God, he has received from the Father the promised Holy Spirit and has poured out what you now see and hear.
- Acts 2:33

The setting of this story was a ten-acre horse ranch on Purgatory Road outside of New Braunfels. I was doing equine therapy with kids from the elementary school that I was working at. This was part of my private practice, and during the summer, they were able to come to do the therapy at the ranch with the horses.

On the ranch I have a house with big windows that lets lots of light in. It was the middle of the day, and I was pacing in the living room that connected to the kitchen. I had been on Facebook and had seen a picture of a former client that I had treated when she was 14 years old as part of her time in foster care. She had practically raised herself and I had the pleasure of developing a relationship with her and her foster mom.

On the day that I saw her picture she had grown to be 23 years old, and God had once again told me that she was part of an assignment from him.

By the post on Facebook, her conversations were very sexual as were her photos. She was on drugs, and she was working in construction work and living with the man that had hired her. One of her friends had called me and told me that she had tried to help her father, who was also on drugs, but instead had been raped by him.

It became evident that God was asking me to intervene with this girl and I was resistant to the idea of taking the project on.

In my house on the ranch, I paced and cried and argued with God. "God, I have raised my kids, I'm tired. Do you know how long it would take to get her cleaned up and educated? I am in my seventies."

In my mind I had convinced God. I went and washed my face and told Him I needed a sign that he understood that I could not take this on. It was hard for me to argue with Him, because He has been so good to me, my Protector, Provider, and a loving Father.

As I look back like a fly on the wall, I am listening to the rantings and ravings of this old woman who is alone in this house in the middle of the woods with the sun coming in from all sides. I was waiting on a sign from God, when my cell phone rings and I pick up and listen to a recording that says, "This is the Dallas Police Department with a collect call from . . .."

This was not the sign I was looking for. God still expected me to tend to her.

THE OLD RANCH ON PURGATORY ROAD

On Purgatory Road on the Devil's Backbone sits a ten-acre horse ranch. The plot of land is rectangular with a white stone three-bedroom two bath house at the end of the property. When my plans to leave El Paso and marry a man from New Braunfels fell through, I remained in the hill country outside of New Braunfels. This ranch was my landing place and home for 27 years.

It must sit on sacred ground, spiritual or American Indian, who knows, after all this is Texas. Texas didn't have boundaries and natives had lived in the area following buffalo and wild horses.

On the back of the house was a wooded area, that had a huge tree with its branches hanging down creating a secret space not noticeable from the road. I had always avoided going into that sacred space. In this space the natural rock had formed a flat shelf like an altar, across the road from the tree was an old gravestone, undisturbed by human hands for many years.

When I first moved onto the ranch the first seven years, I lived in an old double wide home that was on the front 5 acres. I walked the 10 acres of the ranch for many years to find the right spot to build a new home. My favorite memory of this time was watching the 24 baby goats climb the trees to eat the leaves and play around. Because they were black and white, they appeared be tarantulas in the trees.

After seven years of mortgage payments, the woman that sold me the acreage agreed to separate the last two acres for the bank to finance a real house. I knew I wanted the house to be built right in front of a dry creek bed. I knew that during the rainy season, the creek would be full, but my house would be safe. I planned my house with it facing this dry creek bed.

In 2007, I had a huge party in the back yard to celebrate my 65th birthday. Family and friends came from all areas as far as California to attend. My small stone house was full of children running in and out of the house and live music added to the day's festivities. The celebration extended into the night and guests began to leave around midnight. Being out in the country, friends and family members found a place to sleep, to return home the next day.

I was the last one awake and I went out into the backyard to clean the last of the mess. I became aware that something was different, and I felt like I was caught in a bubble.

The night insects were louder, the lightning bugs began to multiply and dance around. It was so enchanting. I felt like I couldn't move. I was mesmerized, my feet were glued to the ground, and time seemed to stand still.

When I was finally released from this bubble, the yard returned to normal, and I was able to walk back into the house. Friends and family were asleep and I felt surrounded by my loved ones. All was well with my world.

This wasn't the only time strange things happened on the ranch. Before my baby sister passed away, I was laying one night in my bed. I had been talking to our mother on the phone and she had shared that Lola was very sick. Lola had suffered with colon canccr for many years and she had come to visit me at the ranch and loved walking around the area. That night as I was thinking about her laying in her own bed in El Paso, I felt her presence come into my bedroom. She climbed into bed with me and snuggled close as though she was cold. I knew it was my sister, but it was still strange to feel her presence when I knew she was sick in El Paso. I slowly slipped out of bed and gave her the bed all to herself.

Another time in my bedroom I was settling in for the night, when I was surprised by a tall man coming into my bedroom. My security alarm was set, but it had not gone off. The man was a young

Indian dressed in a loincloth chasing something, but I couldn't see what it was. He seemed completely unaware I was there. As my mind recognized that the alarm wasn't going off, the Indian disappeared and I was left alone with another sleepless night.

A third time, my then boyfriend was spending the night at the ranch and was already asleep. I was thirsty and hadn't been able to fall asleep so I went into the kitchen to get some water. As I went back into the bedroom, a huge glow appeared above the bed. As my eyes adjusted to the dark, I made out what looked like an angel coming out of my boyfriend's sleeping body. I stood there staring at it frozen in time, it was an angel! A booming voice said, "You can do anything you set your mind to." Then the angel sank back into my boyfriend's body.

The last episode was the one I had the hardest time believing. It was morning and I was still in bed. I was savoring the last minutes under the blanket when I saw a familiar figure enter my bedroom. No warning, no announcement, just the arrival of….

JESUS

walked in and sat on my side of the bed looking out the window where the sun was already out. There was no fanfare, no angels, just my Jesus sitting on the edge of the bed, looking out the window! I sat up and leaned over and placed my head against his shoulder, just for a quiet moment. Then my head fell forward when his shoulder was no longer there to support my head.

I kept this to myself for some time, but slowly I began to share with a few friends.

THREE MEN UNDER GOD'S RADAR

My God not only knows every star's name and position in the sky, but He also knows all our names, our life span, and the plan He has created for each one of us. Most of the time, we don't see the role we play in His Plan.

Because of this, I have learned to ask myself, "What is the lesson for me?"

When I came to San Marcos, I was getting married to a man in New Braunfels 15 minutes away. That fell through and I stayed in San Marcos without any friends. God dropped me here and thus provided for my needs.

In 1995, I met three men. All three were white males in their 50s, and all three I counted as my friend. This strange group of three was bound together only in my mind.

They didn't know each other, and these three men had been my friends in different areas of my life. In a way two of them shared the last years of their lives with me. Each left a lasting impression of who they were and in different ways enriched my life.

Since I didn't know anyone in San Marcos, my social circle began with a couple born and raised here, Liz and Joe Espinoza. Through the Espinoza's, I discovered the surrounding area.

They knew all the Goodwill's and Thrift shops within a 50-mile area. Mr. Espinoza's main interest is old coins and art, and Mrs. Espinosa loves old china and glass. She can recognize different patterns and who manufactures them. She knows what pattern each of her friends has and will buy that pattern as a gift. It is through her that I started my glass pattern, that I now collect. I spent my off time with them for many years.

One year the Espinozas and I were joined by the first man in God's group, Joel. He and the Espinozas had gone to school together and were good friends. He had been living in Houston for years by himself since he retired from the Air Force. His family lived in San Marcos so he sold his house in Houston and bought a condominium in San Marcos. The condominium he bought, he discovered, had a faulty foundation.

Because of this, Joel spent the next five years going through the legal system to recover the money he invested in the condominium. He spent money on lawyers but was not successful in the courts.

Joel's frustrations with the legal system were voiced to us on the occasions he would join us. He was a very intelligent man who didn't have any social skills. His only topic of conversation was politics. One unique time that we were waiting for the Espinozas, I heard about his military experience in the Air Force.

He told me about a very negative experience of discrimination throughout his long term in the military. Because of his low social skills and fixated attention, he had been passed over for promotions and this left him bitter and angry. This combined with the long battle to try to recover the money he had invested in his condominium brought back those feelings. I had not seen just how defeated he felt.

Three months later, April 2014, after having exhausted his monetary resources on court fees, Joel rented a storage unit. He parked the car inside the unit, closed the door, and turned on the car, and committed suicide.

Through Joel, I learned how small life can be. He had traveled all over the world and done so much, but something so simple became overwhelming. He felt like he could no longer deal with it.

The second man, David, I met while working for San Marcos CISD. He was the best second-grade elementary school teacher at Crockett Elementary. On any given day, I never knew what adventure his class would go on, and it wasn't uncommon to find snakes, tarantulas, and mice in his classroom. I was lucky enough to be the elementary school counselor, and I passed his classroom on and off during the day. It was often the highlight of my day.

In God's plan, David remained in my group of friends. Eventually, he started to rent a country house from me. And since he had no family close by, he became part of my family. He would come in with deer meat, sausage, or dessert that he had just baked when my children brought my grandchildren over.

David was my guardian at the ranch, outside San Marcos, where I lived alone for twenty years. Just knowing he rented the front house at the entrance to my property, helped me feel safe.

In time, he bought his own house close by, and I would be invited over or hear from school friends what a great time they had at David's. We were all family.

Much to our surprise in 2003, David was convicted of a federal crime and sentenced to serve ten years in federal prison. One of the teacher aids and I rushed to his side and testified to his good character and standing in the community. He was convicted of the crime and sent to prison in North Carolina. While he was in prison, I handled his finances for him. David earned another master's degree in theology while in prison. The plan was to teach in seminary school after he came out.

After David was released from prison in September 2013, he returned to San Marcos. It was hard for him to find a place to live or a job. He had saved money from the school district, but with paying for his education in prison and buying a car when he came back, the money was running out. In January 2014, David invited all his school friends to lunch and afterward came to my office looking for me. I was not in my office and missed him.

Shortly that day, David sold his car, paid for his own cremation, bought a gun, rented a room in New Braunfels, and killed himself. The police had my address to notify me of his death. The next day I received a letter with his farewell instructions on how to dispose of his belongings. The funeral home had my phone number and they notified me to go pick up his ashes.

David had spent time washing the sheets and his clothes and instructions to donate them to one of his ex-students. I spent the next weekend moving most of his furniture and the clothes to the ex-student's home.

I learned from David, that even up until the end he was considerate of others. He was feeling hopeless, but he still wanted to provide for those he cared about.

It is through my current job as a Licensed Professional Counselors Supervisor (LPC-S) that I met the third man in God's group, John. John had been a school counselor for many years and was my intern to earn his Texas License, to open his own private practice and leave the schools.

John lives with his mother and acts as her caretaker. He is also a pastor at a church in Nixon, Texas. When he left his job at the school district, he started traveling to the different foster homes to do counseling with foster children.

In 2017, he worked with the victims of the church shooting in Sutherland, Texas. After he completed his internship of 3000 hours with me, he became a Licensed Profession Counselor (LPC) by the state of Texas.

He is trying to find his way in his business. Even after he finished his time with me, he still calls often to consult on cases and check on me. I am his mother's age and I know he worries about me.

The way that John won't let me go, has touched my heart.

From God's group, these three men, there is one man still alive. My mantra of, "What's the lesson to these losses?" has been tested these past few years.

I feel like it better be a good lesson because of the cost… immense emotional pain.

I was totally devastated by the passing of those two men that had befriended me at a time that I needed friends. My grief was long and painful because I had lost my mother six months before Joel died.

John doesn't know the story. I wait for his calls when he checks on me but really… do I need to share the story with him?

God doesn't share His plan for you with you. It would be unbelievable to hear God telling you, your complete life story to the end . . . your end. And I believe it would spoil the surprises, shock, or experiences He has in store for you.

Like I shared, "What is the lesson behind this experience?" It better be a good one . . . it cost me a whole mess of pain. One does not lose two friends in such proximity and not worry about the third left alive.

THE MAN I CAN'T FORGIVE

My heart is always overwhelmed by God's generosity and my life is so blessed, so full of people that I love.

On a regular day, I found myself going to check my mail at the UPS store. Not being aware of my surroundings, I just want to hurry and get my mail.

One of the million things that keeps me busy keeping Gods business going. In my preoccupation, I don't notice a stranger until she touches me, and I stop and look up.

The older woman is wearing a mask, all I can see is her eyes. They are so full of love. I look deeper as if into a cave.

My being comes to life...my own love, delight, matches hers! This is my child that has been lost to me for years. I recognize her! Everything in the room blurs, I hug her. Both of us hug tightly! I can't believe it. I found someone I had lost to death.

But here she is! In the next few minutes, which to me was an eternity, I would hug her, then touch her, look at her, not believing my eyes. Touch her, look at her and touch her again. Her name is on my lips, Miriam. A lifetime ago I met Miriam. My sweet young woman.

But a hundred years later, here she is, in front of me. Alive. In between the last hundred years, Miriam has called me. The phone will ring late in the night. I will hear a familiar voice. But my familiar voice is missing the spark of life.

"How are the girls? How is Junior? "I will ask.

The phone conversation is missing something. Her spirit, her energy is not there. She's reaching out to me, a memory out of her past.

During the conversation I will check her vitals, "Are you driving? How's the store? Are you still in the back house?"

I met Miriam more than twenty-five years ago. She was a young girl then, the same age as one of my daughters. As a therapist I saw her once a week. She was depressed but functioning. She had two girls and two boys. Junior was a little boy at that time.

She was married to a young man who was openly unfaithful to her. He had a successful business with men working for him. He repeatedly told her of his plan for building a house in Mexico, leaving her, and going to live with the same woman he has been cheating on her for years. At one point Mariam found out that the woman was pregnant with her husband's child.

Her depression that was fueled by her husband's unfaithfulness grew deeper and deeper. She wrote many journals on her own depression and her own thoughts. Miriam wrote a book, **Because You Cared** about me as her therapist and her thoughts as we worked in our sessions.

She had it bounded and presented it to me. Alongside the book, she wrote a poem to me, printed it and framed it.

How could I not be surprised to see her again? "Once she was lost and now, she's found".

Somewhere in our phone talks, I heard her tell me how she couldn't put her thoughts together to even write. Writing is her soul… her life force.

Miriam was figuring out life one printed page at a time. She told me of the countless number of journals she kept in the attic. In my office I myself hold several lifetimes of tears and despair that she has experienced. Miriam is an old soul.

At that time, I had a home on 10 acres in the country and she came to stay at my place for several days. She gave me instructions to let her work on herself, and at night I would hear her crying and talking to herself. At the end of that time, she had figured out whatever had been troubling her.

For the next five years or so she started a store selling religious articles and was very successful. She volunteered at the church and started a support group. She would also visit sick people in their homes.

I gave a sigh of relief. She was done with therapy.

A couple of times she brought lunch into the office, and we talked. Miriam and I had worked together for years and were connected so she would bring me messages at the office.

One time she came to my office and said, "I had a dream and was told that you need money and would never ask."

She extended an envelope from the bank with two thousand dollars. Two of my clients, not related to each other, were having financial problems ready to be evicted from their homes. I had been referring them to local agencies but still no help. The money went to those two clients, a thousand dollars each. Miriam's husband owns a big business and could afford to donate the money even though he was unaware of the donation. She wouldn't take no for an answer.

Miriam came many times with similar messages for me. We lost touch for several years. Then one night, late as usual, she called. Something was wrong! Her thoughts were incomplete and disconnected, slurred, not herself.

I began assessing her, "Are you driving? Writing another book?"

She didn't seem to know what I was talking about. My phone number was in her phone. My face came to her, and she called. She had had a stroke. I learned that Miriam was also afraid to go out of her home, afraid of people.

"My sweet, sweet Miriam, "I cried. What did he do to you? I couldn't stop crying. "Don't you remember the book you wrote? "I pleaded with her. Her silence at the other end of the phone was her response.I was crying silently for the loss of …. words…thoughts… Miriam's soul. Her contribution to the world as an author was lost.

Now all these years later, the couple coming out of the UPS store was Miriam and her husband. I shook his hand, and he went to the car to wait for Miriam. When she had the stroke, he turned out to be her caretaker.

Some years earlier Miriam's husband had come to the office for therapy. His idea of running off with the other woman was shattered when Miriam suffered the stroke.

Another victim of his fantasy had been his 15-year-old son who had heard the stories throughout the years. When Miriam had the stroke, her son who had had mental problems during those years, had a nervous breakdown.

One morning as his father was in the kitchen cleaning up, the distraught son tried to stab him several times. Miriam's husband came to my office for treatment of trauma sometime after. He survived and his son is in prison.

He would later claim that he had envisioned Jesus forgiving him. He smiled as he told the story of hearing Jesus's voice.

I was angry! I have not forgotten all the years of Miriam's anguish and neglect! I have not forgotten her years of being lost in her mind trying to figure out why her husband couldn't love her. My mind couldn't forget years of Miriam's tears and depression.

Miriam is not able to function because of the years of verbal abuse, his verbal abuse. And now his son was added to the list of victims.

Our Father

"……forgive us our trespasses as we forgive those who trespass against us."

God asks us to forgive others but as humans we can't forget. As a human therapist I believe that forgiveness is a process. As God's child, I ask for forgiveness for believing so. I believe that tending to our pain comes first. I guess that is why I'm a therapist, to tend to the pain of the emotion and allow the process to go through. I say, "forgiveness takes time" in my office. I work with people, God's children.

A hundred years have passed, and I am working on forgiving Miriam's husband. Forgetting takes time. God, God, I can't forgive this man for destroying Miriam's life and their family.

A week later Miriam and I met for lunch after church. Her husband drove her to the restaurant and dropped her off.

As soon as we were seated, I started with my assessment. I had not seen her since her stroke when she couldn't put words together. "Can you drive? How are the kids? Are you writing? What has he done to you?"

Miriam smiled and said, "he has come full circle. Since the stroke, he has taken care of me. He cooks and feeds me, cleans the house, and washes clothes. He does everything. He cries and asks me to forgive him "how could I have hurt you? ". We talk about the past.

Two hours later, Miriam's husband comes to pick her up.

As they drive off, I realize how the week has gone for me.

I have spent several days writing Miriam's story, crying the whole time. Days of anger towards her husband and compassion for her.

God's timing was perfect, when He directed them for a box at the UPS store, where I ran into them. A whole week of waiting for the lunch date with Miriam, where she reports "he has come full circle".

God's Plan was for me!! I am still working on forgiveness!

Psalm 32.5. Then I acknowledged my sin to you and did not cover up my iniquity. I said, "I will confess my transgressions to the Lord"- and you forgave the guilt of my sin.

RELEASED

My escape has been coming for the last year or so. I feel empowered, but at the same time, I feel like a baby chick breaking the eggshell at my age. I have released my constant companion in the egg, my ex-husband, for we're still connected by anger.

My 14-year marriage with three children ended in 1979. The emotional abuse had taken its toll. The quiet, shy girl that had gotten married in 1963 was now the mother of three and ready to protect.

She was prepared to flee. I was afraid of the dark, but I slept on the recliner in the living room when my husband was out. On the recliner, I could keep an eye on the back door, the front door, and the hallway where my babies slept.

Fourteen years had changed me, and it didn't feel good. I could verbally protect myself and my children. I was proud of expressing myself without four-letter words. Now in my office as a professional therapist, I explain how anger can be an ally.

Anger kept me safe when I was afraid. Anger protected me when my feelings were being stepped on. At 32, I ended up with a shield around me and my children, ready to fight anyone! It didn't feel good. The shy girl had become a watchdog.

After 14 years of this marriage, I called my father to get my children and me. I took my shield with me into the wilderness, the world. I was 32 years old, and with the help of my faith in God, my parents, and my sisters, I've come into my seventies.

My experiences in the wilderness held everything good and evil, scary and familiar, falling out of grace with my God and finally accepting His Guidance.

Like my poem in my first book:

The Question

How did these magnificent souls choose me as their mother?

For they came after I existed,

Thus, they chose me.

They raised me to what I am now,

Not the other way around.

For they turned on the color,

Onto a black and white canvas.

For I was painted on a wall,

Without breath or meaning.

My anger and my shield protected me, and I kept them close by! My ex-lives on his side of the world in El Paso, and I live 650 miles away. The eggshell I dragged along...my anger. I have carried him connected by anger for 42 years. Out of sight, out of mind. My trigger can't bother me.

I became a teacher, a counselor, a therapist. A significant part of my practice is women breaking up, divorcing, and separating. The young 32-year-old in my shell is always listening and learning... and maturing.

Well, God stepped in about two months ago. In February, the heavy snowstorm that trapped me in my home for a week without electricity AND without work pushed me to think about the only part in my life that holds anger, my eggshell where I carry my ex.

Wednesday of that week, feeling low and nowhere to go, the black door in the back of my mind that had been shut for 42 years opened. That released all the ugly memories repressed since my divorce.

The therapist in me couldn't figure out what was happening. My ex wasn't in my space! He had always been the trigger that brought the anger to the surface. I realized that God had lost his patience with me! My crying was so hard that I couldn't breathe!

I wasn't the therapist! I was the young 32-year-old releasing 14 years of abuse. To protect my three children, I had shut the door and put on my shield for 42 years.

On that icy day, my memories were released to process the divorce of so long ago. The grief for the loss of my marriage had never come to be. My survival wasn't possible without the energy of the anger. The shield had held me together all my adult life. But the same shield kept me from allowing loving relationships in. Another poem from my first book:

> "Oh, heartless heart-what do you feel?
>
> You keep on beating-and yet so still.
>
> There was a shell so hard and high
>
> To keep you going… to keep you safe."

I called my friend that I had met at training years before. She led me through an exercise that stabilized me that day. Once the 32-year-old felt better, God broke through, carrying his miraculous response, **Compassion!**

God continued to put a picture of us when we were dating in my mind. God was reframing my concept of a lifetime. We had the marriage of two kids wanting out of their family of origin, but neither had held any love for each other. We had not known each other long enough to form a relationship. We met in June and married in September. I had said, "I will marry the first guy that has a job and a car." My ex had been running to Mexico the night before our wedding. Not the best foundation for a marriage.

God was working on me to get rid of my anger and keep on doing his work. Compassion for the two kids that got married, my ex and me.

That was February of this year 2021. I'm a work in progress. My first book was about my grief trying to come out. Even my creativity was trapped in my shield.

After writing this, I joined my ex for a family celebration at my daughter's house. I have finally let him go. My eggshell, anger is slowly dissipating.

BENEVOLENT FATHER

As a therapist I sit in the front-row seat next to Father. I get the feeling of a well-planned lesson carried out through time and space. In my mind's eye, I see the story unfold.

Luis and Anna

They could be any young couple in the 50s. A tall, dark, and handsome young man meets a smart and beautiful girl. She is attracted to the strong, dominant young man. Their life unfolds together, and they marry and live out their 60-year-old-marriage and are now in their 80s.

Throughout the years, Luis's dominant trait has paid off, and his business is worth a couple of millions. With Anna behind him as his business partner, they have prospered into a well-known family in their town.

The strong, dominant man Anna chose has grown to be controlling and abusive. As the years passed, she has taken on a different role as Luis became more and more abusive. As she ages, she needs a cane to keep her balance and not fall.

Their life together has been the culmination of 4 children: two boys and two girls, raised and refined in a catholic setting. They live on their land, surrounded by acres where four other houses have also been built by them. One daughter lives in one house. The sons are well-educated and live in Round Rock and San Antonio. The fourth child, Linda, does her own thing.

"I am the black sheep of the family," says Linda. She has led her life apart from the family in the same small town. Linda has had several long relationships, including one with her ex-husband Miguel, whom she has two daughters with. They divorced but share several grandchildren. Being involved in her girls' lives, Linda still includes her ex-husband and ex mother-in-law in her life.

The other relationships have left their mark on Linda, because she has followed in her mother's footsteps, and she has chosen strong, dominant, and handsome men. She has lived an emotionally abusive life. As she gets older, the break-ups are more severe and take longer to recover. This late breakup in the last two years has taken a toll on Linda.

From my observation position, I can see the big picture of God's (Father)Plan and how all factors come into play to benefit all concerned.

The grand scene started to come together a few weeks ago. Linda was very comfortable at her place. She is adept at setting up a safe place and working on healing from the last relationship.

Linda had been keeping an eye on her mother's health and could see that her mother was not doing well. But every time that she visited her parents, dominant Luis (father) would not talk to her or was rude. Anna also was very rude, and Linda would run home to her safe place to cry.

Then the landlord at her place needed money and pressured Linda for the rent before it was due. Linda hasn't been working for 18 months because of her emotional state of mind. The landlord had also placed Linda in an awkward position. If anyone on the property needed a ride to work, he suggested Linda, because she has a car.

Linda began looking for a place to live. A long-time friend offered her his apartment, where he lived with his brother. She packed all her belongings in her car and moved in with the two brothers. In her depression, she slept for a couple of days. The two men decided that they didn't want Linda there and asked her to leave. Again, she packed all her stuff in her car and made sure that her parents didn't know the bind she was in. She had no place to go.

Linda's mother wasn't feeling well, and she spent a few days in the hospital. Linda was really worried about her mother. Her siblings were also worried but involved in their own lives.

As Linda's therapist, I am sitting next to my Father as an observer and marvel as His Plan unfolds. With all of Linda's siblings busy with their lives and Linda healing from her breakup, she accepts her mother's request to come and be her caretaker.

"I can't do it." Linda declares, "I've been on my own and independent for so long. I love my mother, but I can't live under my father's roof! He locks the doors at 8:00 pm and I must be in, or I get locked out!"

Linda might be the only child in the family that can see how much care her mother needs. Linda also doesn't have another place to go. She had slept in her car the last few days.

After expressing her doubts about living in the family home with her controlling father, Linda moved in. Her concern for her mother's health was much bigger. The next two weeks, Linda learned how to bathe her mother. She would get her out of bed, where she spent most of her days, and gave her little projects to work on. A new recipe, a walk around the garden, Linda had her mother singing and laughing.

As the women sang and laughed, Luis's jealousy or loss of control over his wife took over! He walked over to Linda and got in her face. Linda stood up to her father and said, "Dad, you don't scare me anymore!"

Linda's recent memory was from a couple of years ago. Her father, disagreeing with a remark that she said, walked over and pulled her by the hair. Linda was shocked with being in her fifties and being pulled by her hair like a child.

Today was the same. Her father didn't like Linda and her mother laughing and having a good time, so he got in Linda's face. Anna moved fast and raised her cane. She lowered the cane and cussed Luis out. At the same time, she pushed the cane roughly against Luis' shoulder.

She was defending her daughter!

Ann then added insult to injury. In Spanish, Anna reminded Luis, "I made this business what it is!"

Linda was taken back. She has had enough drama the last few years and she doesn't want anymore. "I can't do this!"

Linda and I had a session with her saying, "I don't know, I don't know!"

"Linda, Linda, who could arrange all these issues together and accomplish so much?" I reminded her, "GOD.

You are valued highly by your mother. Look around, who else has your mother picked to take care of her. It's part of your healing."

Anna the smart, beautiful girl sees herself at the end of her life and she doesn't want to die as a weak and abused wife. She has seen her daughter struggling for years. By standing by Linda, she has again proven to herself how strong she is.

One week became two and toward the fourth week, Linda has proven to be a great caretaker for her mother. But mother has swung back to the position she has always taken…beside her husband. Between the two rude and non-caring parents, Linda stays in her bedroom to avoid conflict. She is the caretaker to her mother and housekeeper of the grand family home.

Linda's siblings come over to see their parents and take them out to lunch or dinner. She is not invited. At times she becomes the family joke, the parents and siblings being rude and disrespecting Linda.

Linda cannot cook in the kitchen, for Luis has control of his kitchen. She must eat out or watch every step she takes in Luis' kitchen. Everything has its place, and everything must be placed exactly where it was. The stress of being back at home has driven Linda into heavier drinking. She will sneak in a bottle of wine, whisky, anything to help her sleep. If she goes out during the day, she is reminded to be back by 7:00 or be locked out. Linda is back to her lifelong position, the black sheep of the family.

Linda bought her mother some flowers and placed them in the living room and again mother ignored the gift her daughter had given her. Linda cried most of the day in her room after getting her mother bathed and set for the day.

The parents sitting in the living room and Linda in her bedroom. When her sister came to see her mother, the two women would make jokes at Linda's expense. "I love my mother. But I cannot stay here!" Linda cried.

She would get on her car, with clothes in the back seat, and drive around the hill country. At times she would park on some dirt road and pray. The young party girl, now 58, had been ostracized by the whole family. The old couple was refusing to support her when she most needed it.

The breaking point came when Luis had had a couple of beers and was rude to Linda. Linda said, "I'm not afraid of you father!" Luis replied angrily, "You better be afraid... Cabrona...you have no father, "pulling out a switchblade and grabbing Linda by the hair. She ran to her room and packed her belongings in the car. They wanted her out. Her mother was not getting into this argument.

She didn't know where she was going. And as she went by the pretty bouquet of flowers she had so lovingly bought for her mother; she picked up the vase and smashed it on the floor and scattered the flowers all over the floor. She slept in her car that night...

Linda couldn't sleep and got up early to figure out what was next. her parents had thrown her out of the grand family home. Her mother had betrayed her! She had rejoined her husband, leaving Linda on her own, out on the streets. "I don't know, I don't know", Linda's usual thought expressed out loud.

Linda had heard of a government program for the homeless during the pandemic. She never thought she would end up there. By the end of the afternoon, she was in one of the several hotels being paid for by the government for families that had lost their jobs and had no income. Small bedroom on the second floor with a window overlooking the parking lot. The television set didn't work but Linda had a laptop. It had a small cooler. Linda would end up living in this small room for the next four months.

Linda had a roof over her head and out of the rain, but she couldn't step outside the door. Groups from the community would come into the hotel offering the occupants (homeless) free food, free clothes. The men who were without jobs had nothing to do but sit around and drink beer all day. Every day. The children would run out in the hallways. Linda made sure her door was locked. But someone still came in a stole her tennis shoes and her purse. Later the desk clerk returned her purse. Empty of any contents.

God make me the instrument of your love. Where there is… hurt, let there be love.

My ears as Linda's therapist were ready several times a day to hear, "I can call the police and report that my dad pulled my hair! He pulled a switchblade on me! I am 58 years old! I am not a child! I can put his ass in jail!"

Linda's mother made several calls a day to say, "you're not that great a mother!" No mercy. The days were long and hard for her. Sobbing, she would again and again say "I don't know, I don't know!" She would sleep days at end. Pray days at end. Four months, four months…

The dirty hotel, the questionable people around, some were selling drugs and Linda knew them from the community.

But God's Plan and God's timing paid off for Linda.

Linda made friends around the community. Bernice, a friend from school became part of Linda's support system. Tanya giving her a job in Wimberley. Cynthia inviting her to church, making Linda's faith stronger and listening to her.

Thanksgiving 2021 came. It was painful to watch Linda remember the last 20 Thanksgivings. She would be invited to the family Thanksgivings and be reminded of all the mistakes she had made in her life and the parents and siblings laughing. But this Thanksgiving would be different, so she thought. Wished. Linda had made up her mind to skip the invitation to the family Thanksgiving this year. She was done with her family!

www.ingramcontent.com/pod-product-compliance
Lightning Source LLC
LaVergne TN
LVHW021304080526
838199LV00090B/6004